2018 USA Calendar – Alaska Nature Photos

(Full Moon Dates = ☺)

Copyright © 2017 Daniel H. Wieczorek & Kazuya Numazawa

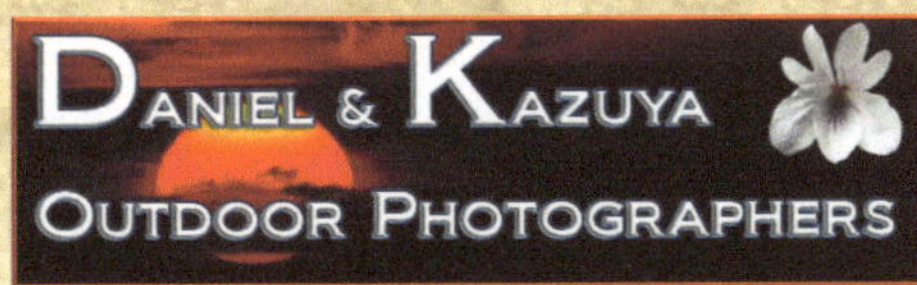

ISBN-10: 0-9969810-5-5
ISBN-13: 978-0-9969810-5-7

PHOTOS INCLUDED IN THIS CALENDAR

January: A Fata Morgana mirage at sunset time (4:08 PM) near Fairbanks, Alaska.
February: A large cow moose (*Alces alces*) near Fairbanks, Alaska.
March: A highly manipulated photo showing Denali (Mt. McKinley) from the George Parks Hwy. near Fairbanks, Alaska.
April: A pair of Sandhill Cranes (*Grus Canadensis*) at Creamer's Field, Fairbanks, Alaska.
May: Calypso Orchids (*Calypso bulbosa* var. *americana*) near Fairbanks, Alaska.
June: *Pedicularis lanata* (Woolly lousewort) at Eagle Summit near Central, Alaska.
July: A Hoary Marmot (*Marmota caligata*) at Table Top Mountain near Chatanika, Alaska.
August: *Vaccinium uliginosum* (Blueberries) at Wickersham Dome near Fairbanks, Alaska.
September: The Aurora Borealis, or Northern Lights near Fairbanks, Alaska.
October: Bearberry (*Arctostaphylos alpina*) on Wickersham Dome near Fairbanks, Alaska.
November: An amazing November morning in the birch forest, Fairbanks, Alaska.
December: Chena Hot Springs Resort on a cold December morning, near Fairbanks, Alaska.

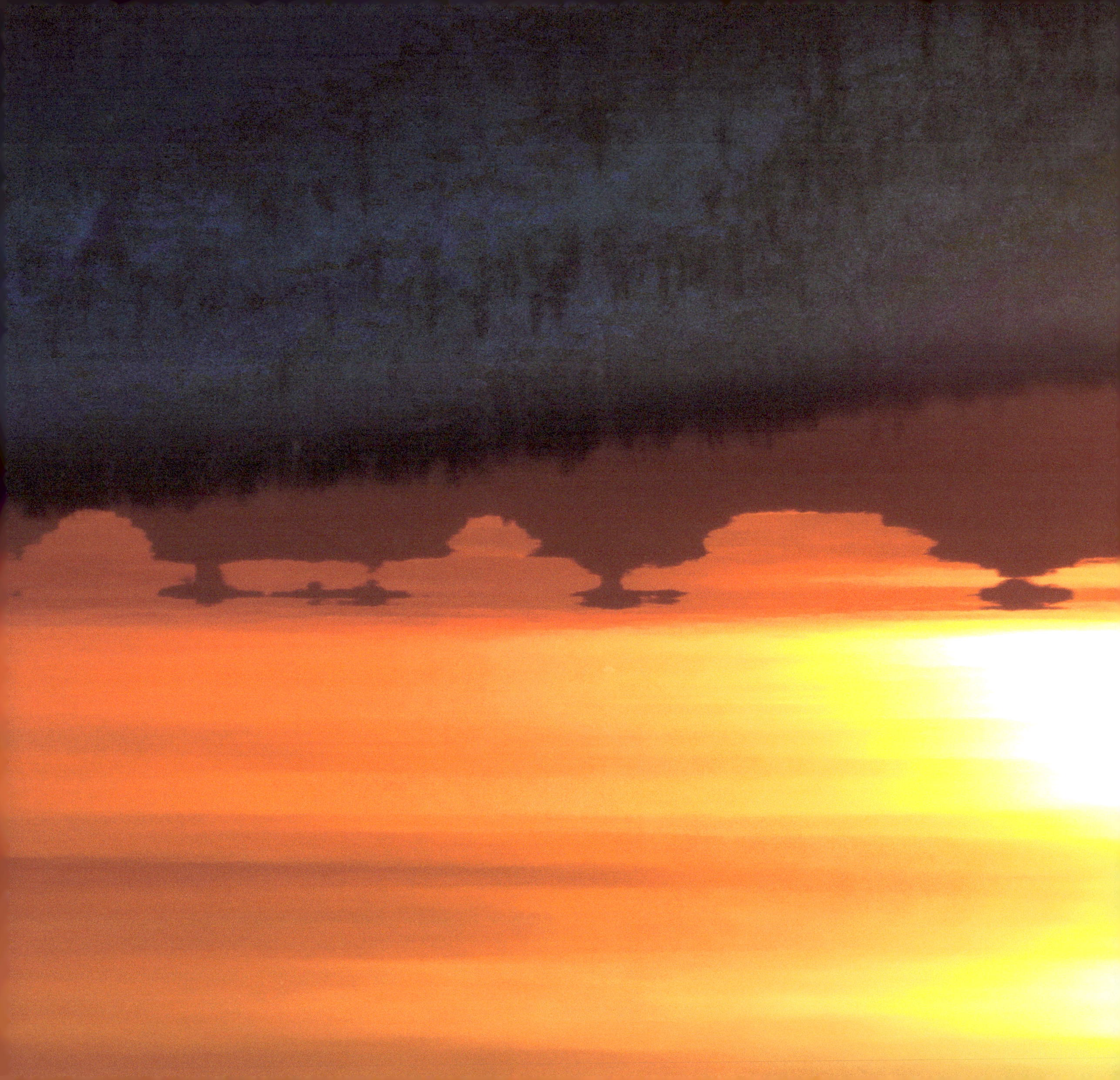

January 2018

Sun	Mon	Tue	Wed	Thu	Fri	Sat
24	25	26	27	28	29	30
31	1 New Year's Day	2	3	4	5	6
7	8	9	10	11	12	13
14	15 Martin Luther King Day	16	17	18	19	20
21	22	23	24	25	26	27
28	29	30	31	1	2	3

A Fata Morgana mirage at sunset time (4:08 PM) near Fairbanks, Alaska.

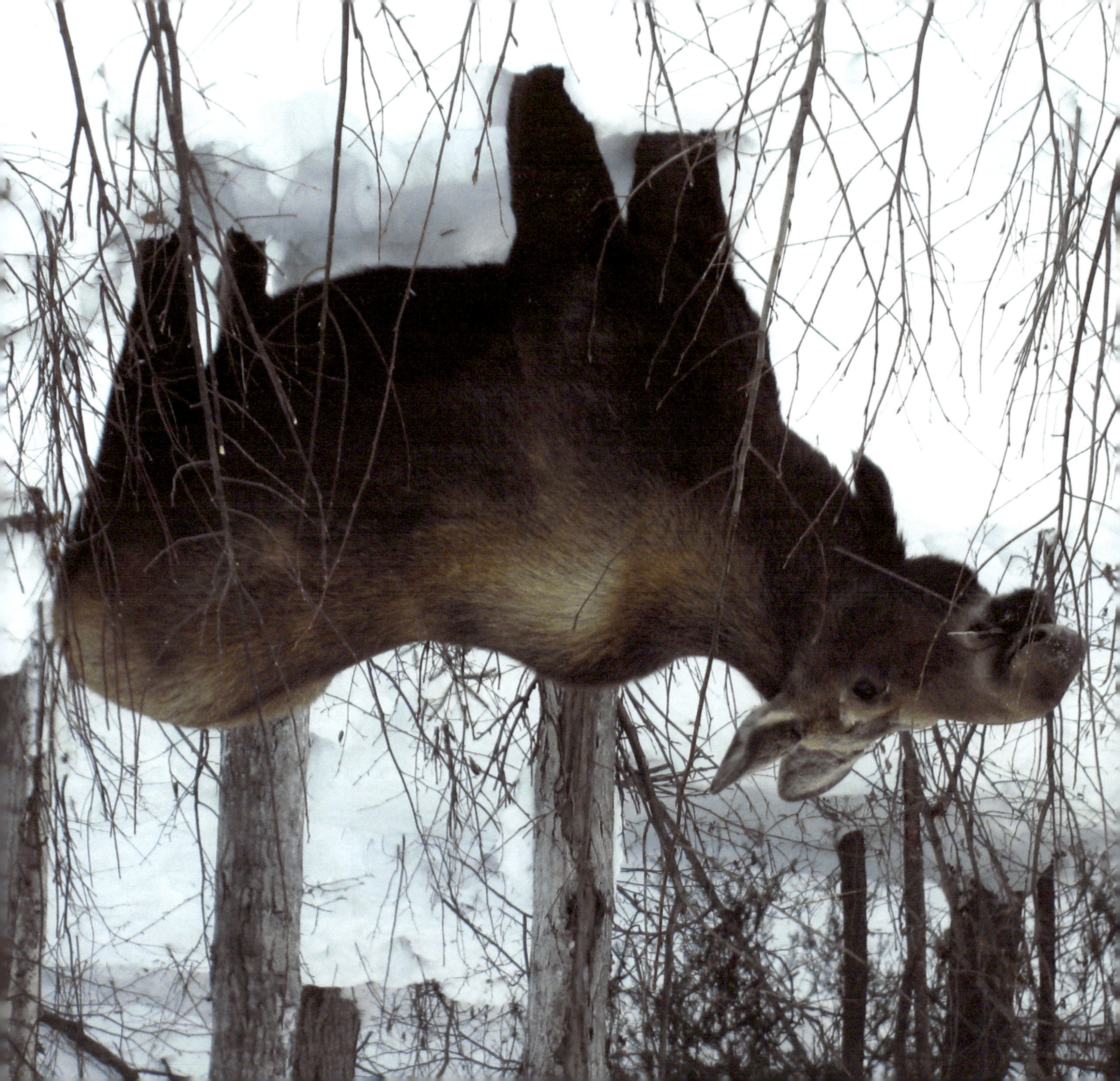

Sun	Mon	Tue	Wed	Thu	Fri	Sat
28	29	30	31	1	2	3
4	5	6	7	8	9	10
11	12	13	14 Valentine's Day	15	16	17
18	19 President's Day	20	21	22	23	24
25	26	27	28	1	2	3

A large cow moose (*Alces alces*) near Fairbanks, Alaska.

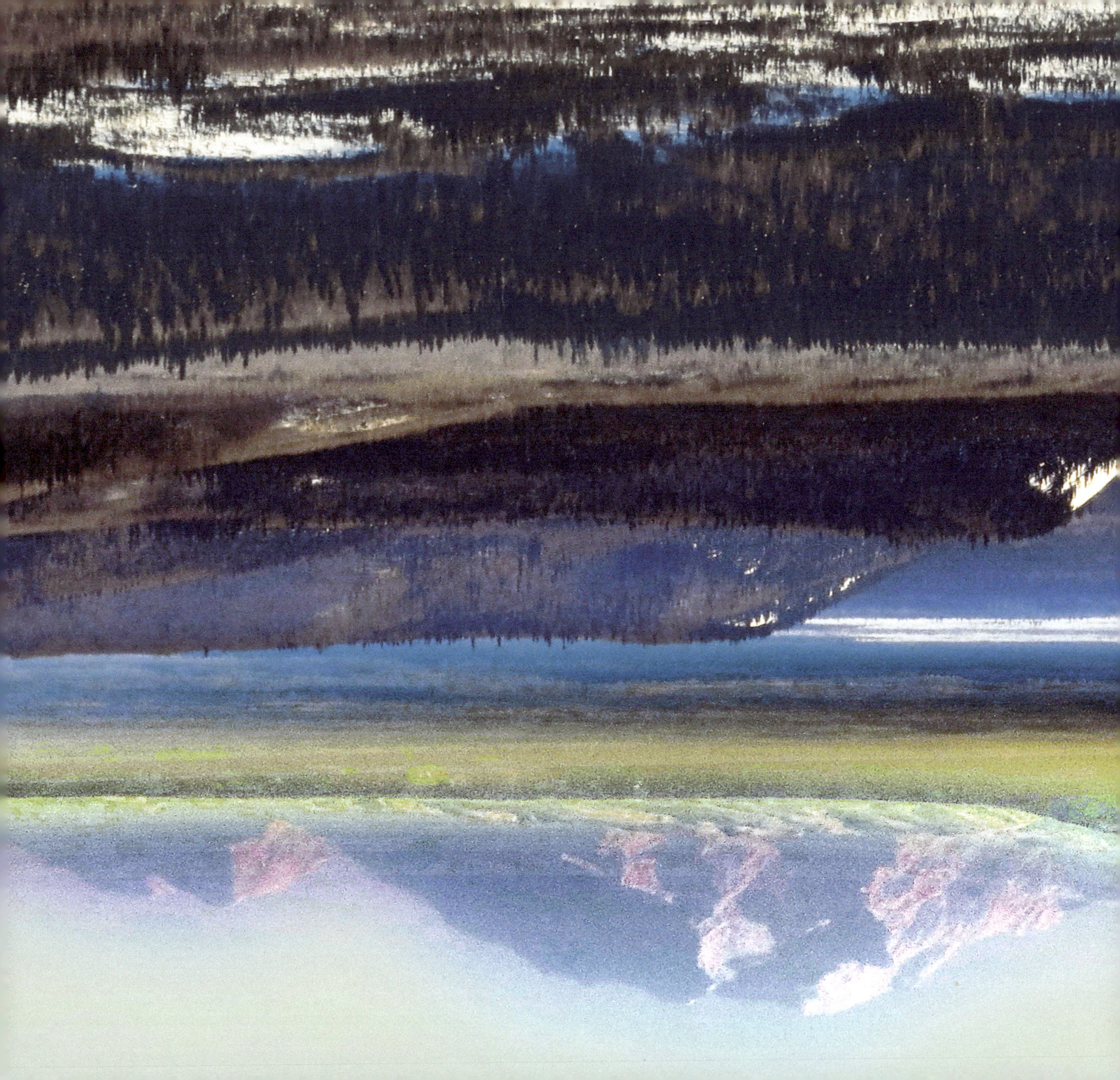

March 2018

Sun	Mon	Tue	Wed	Thu	Fri	Sat
25	26	27	28	☺	2	3
4	5	6	7	8	9	10
11 **Daylight Saving Time Begin (02:00)**	12	13	14	15	16	17
18	19	20 **16:15 GMT Vernal Equinox**	21	22	23	24
25	26	27	28	29	30	31

A highly manipulated photo showing Denali (Mt. McKinley) from the George Parks Highway near Fairbanks, Alaska.

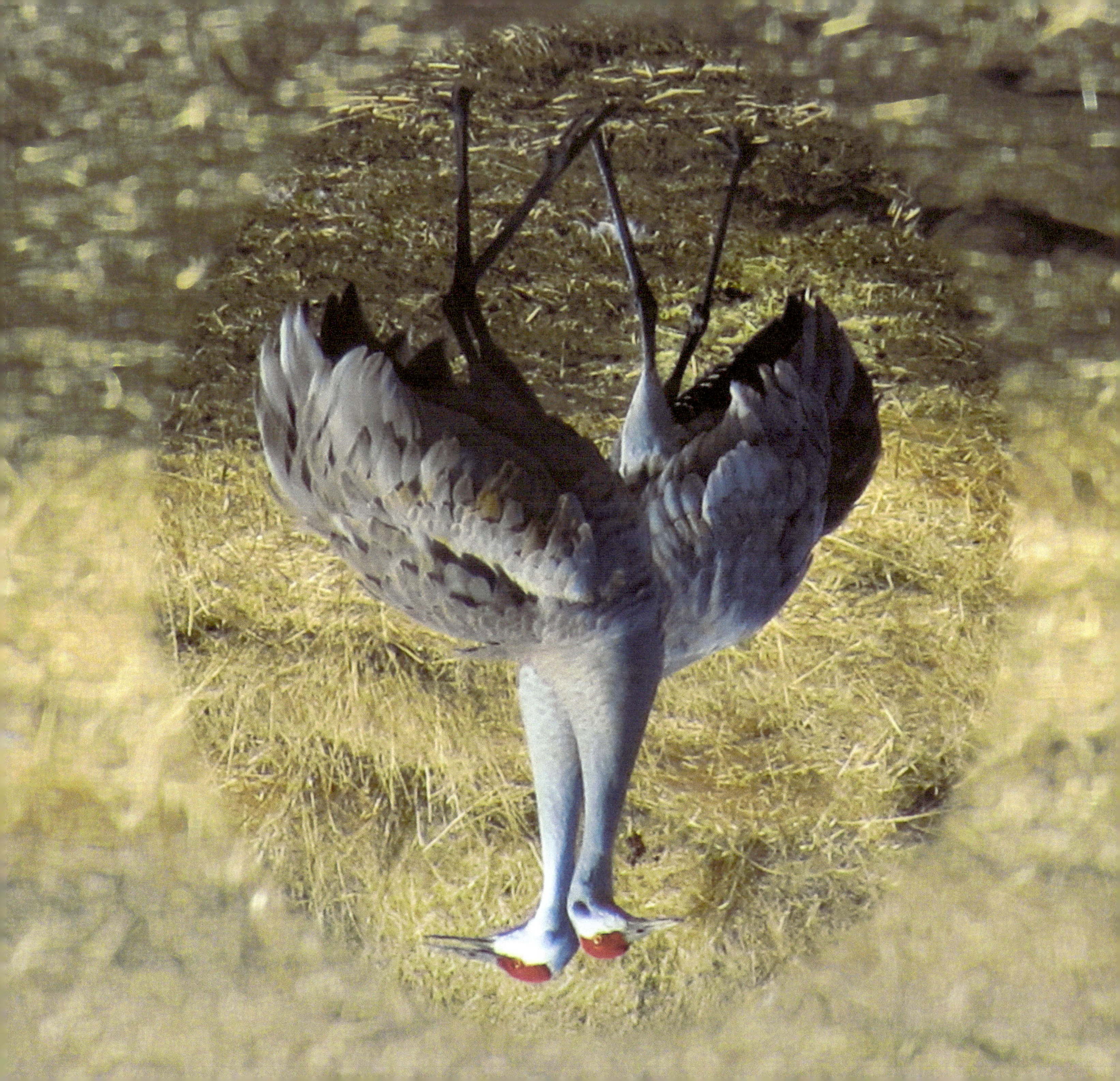

April 2018

Sun	Mon	Tue	Wed	Thu	Fri	Sat
25	26	27	28	29	30	31
1 Easter Sunday	2	3	4	5	6	7
8	9	10	11	12	13	14
15	16	17	18	19	20	21
22	23	24	25	26	27	28
	30	1	2	3	4	6

A pair of Sandhill Cranes (*Grus Canadensis*) at Creamer's Field, Fairbanks, Alaska.

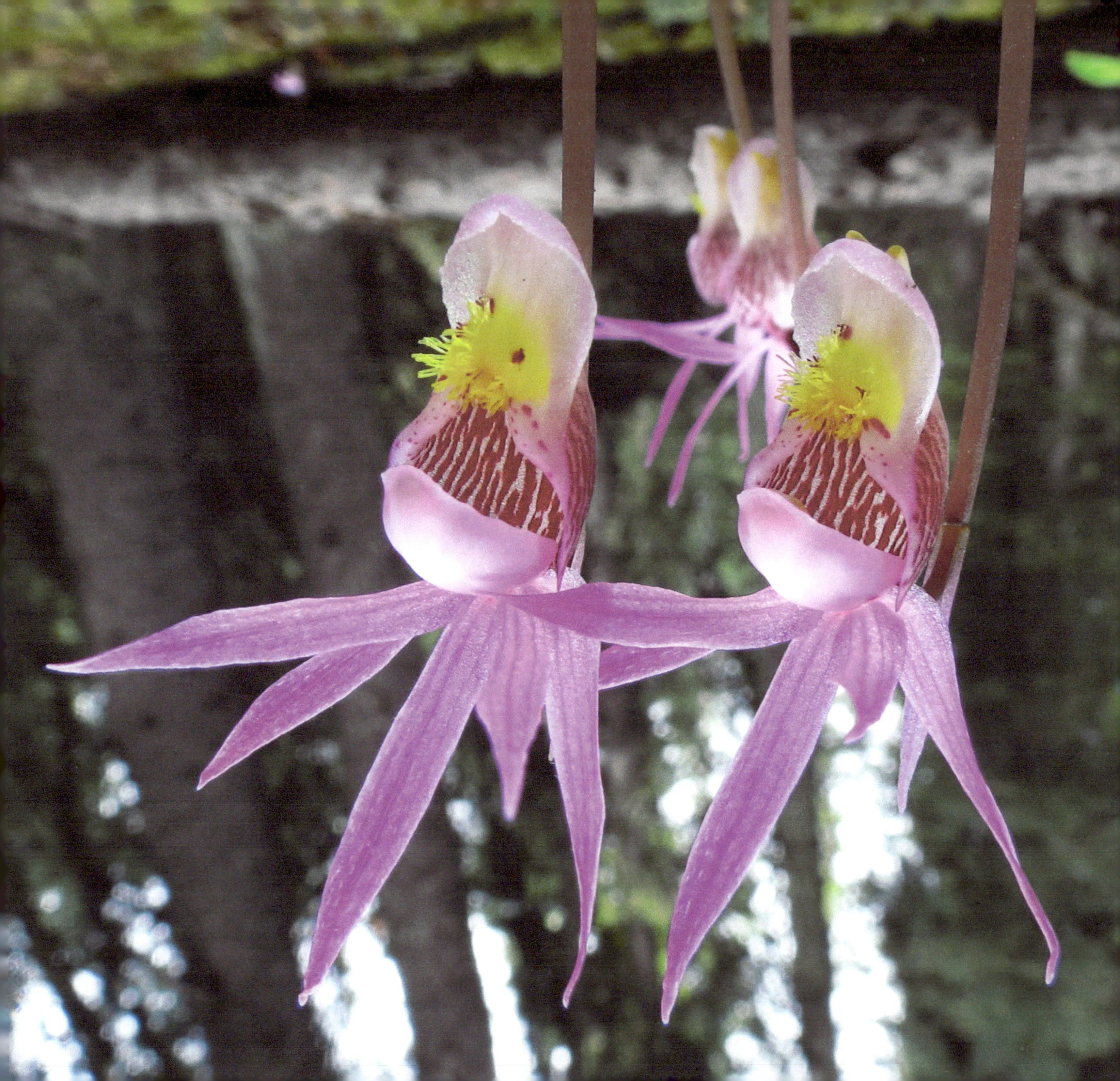

May 2018

Sun	Mon	Tue	Wed	Thu	Fri	Sat
29	30	1	2	3	4	5
6	7	8	9	10	11	12
13 Mother's Day	14	15	16	17	18	19
20	21	22	23	24	25	26
27	28 Memorial Day	☺ 29	30	31	1	2

Calypso Orchids (*Calypso bulbosa* var. *americana*) near Fairbanks, Alaska.

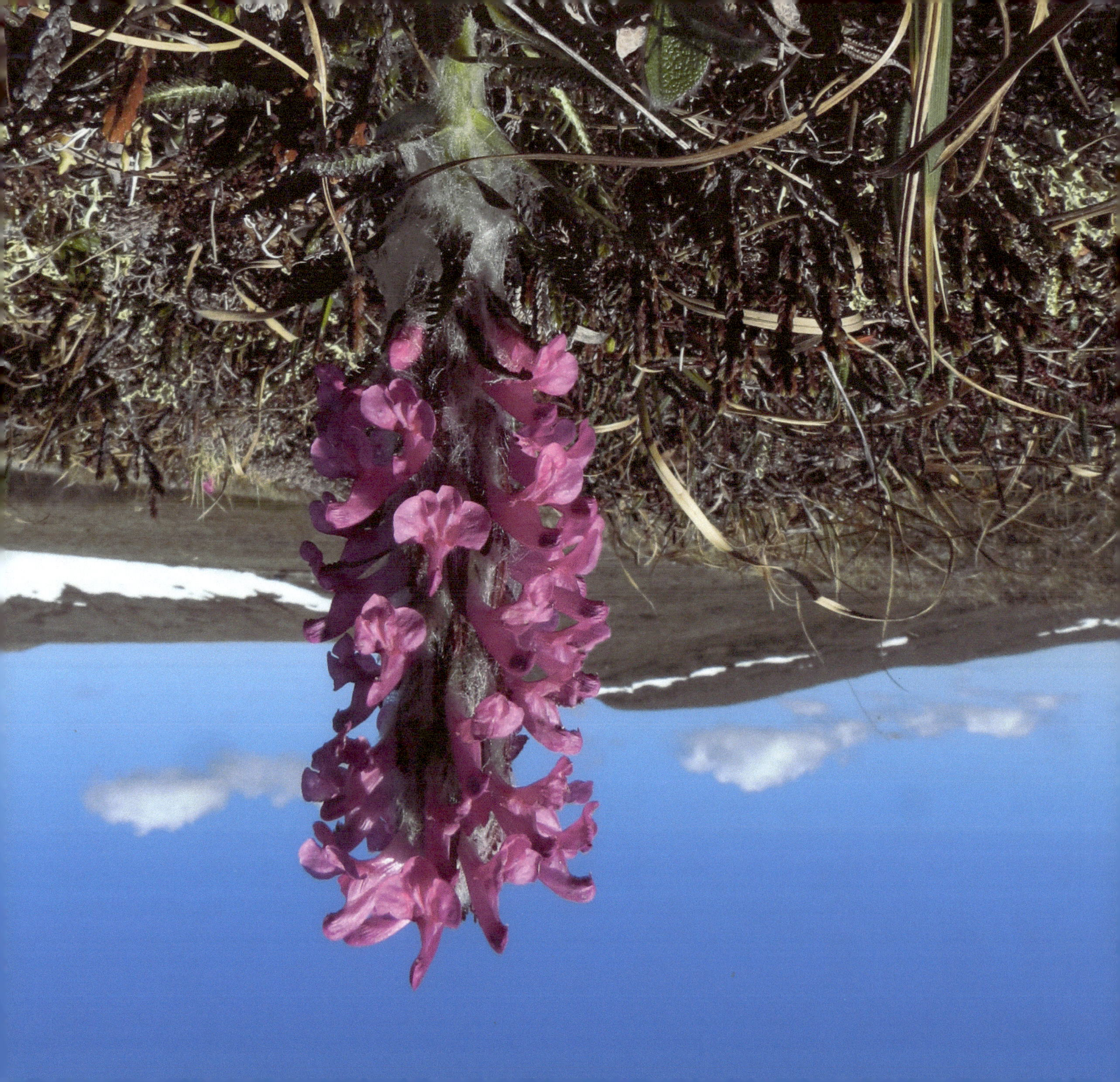

June 2018

Sun	Mon	Tue	Wed	Thu	Fri	Sat
27	28	29	30	31	1	2
3	4	5	6	7	8	9
10	11	12	13	14	15	16
17 Father's Day	18	19	20	21 10:07 GMT Summer Solstice	22	23
24	25	26	27	28	29	30

Pedicularis lanata (Woolly lousewort) at Eagle Summit near Central, Alaska.

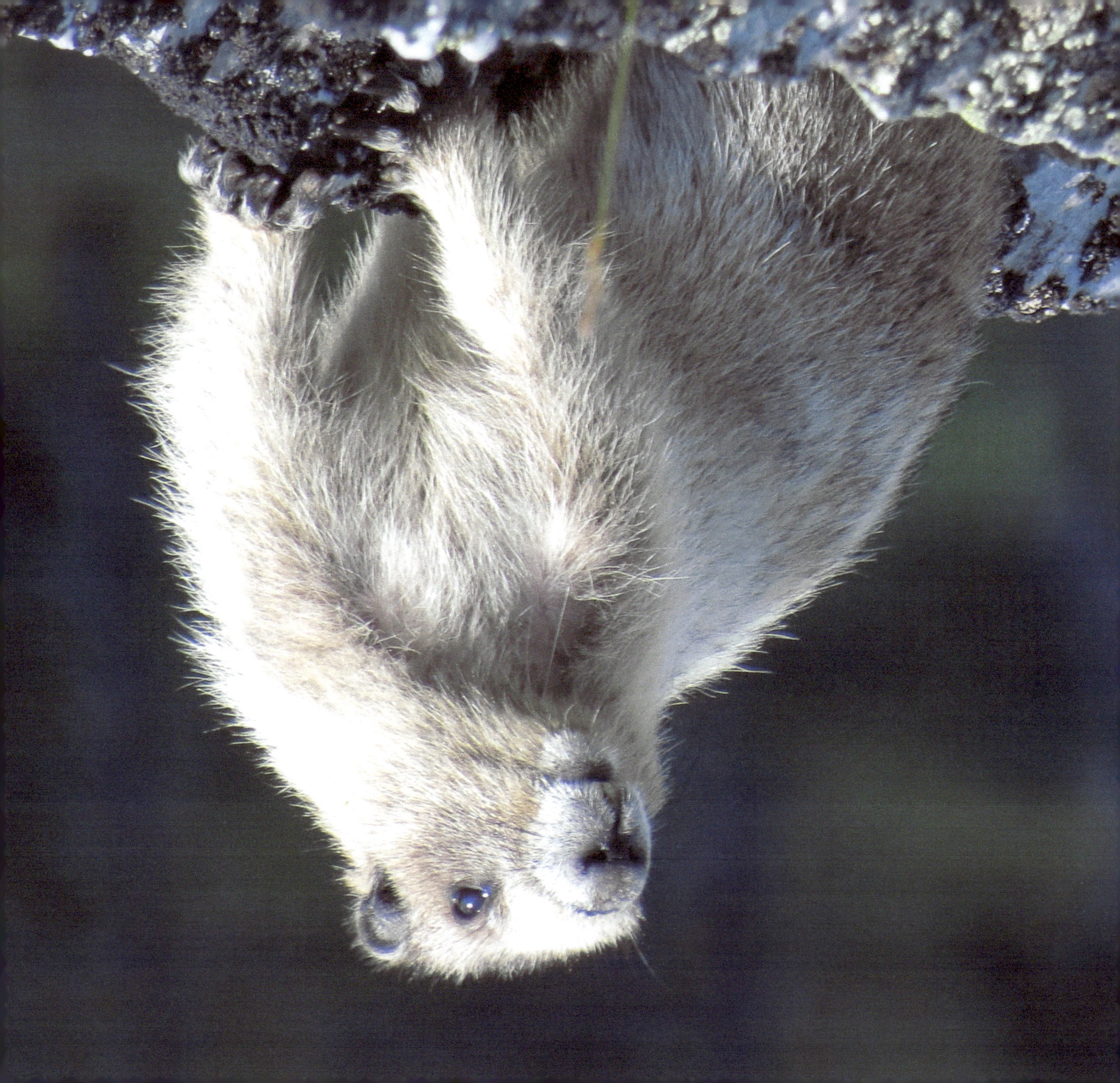

July 2018

Sun	Mon	Tue	Wed	Thu	Fri	Sat
24	25	26	27	28	29	30
1	2	3	4 Independence Day	5	6	7
8	9	10	11	12	13	14
15	16	17	18	19	20	21
22	23	24	25	26	☺	28
29	30	31	1	2	3	4

A Hoary Marmot (*Marmota caligata*) at Table Top Mountain near Chatanika, Alaska.

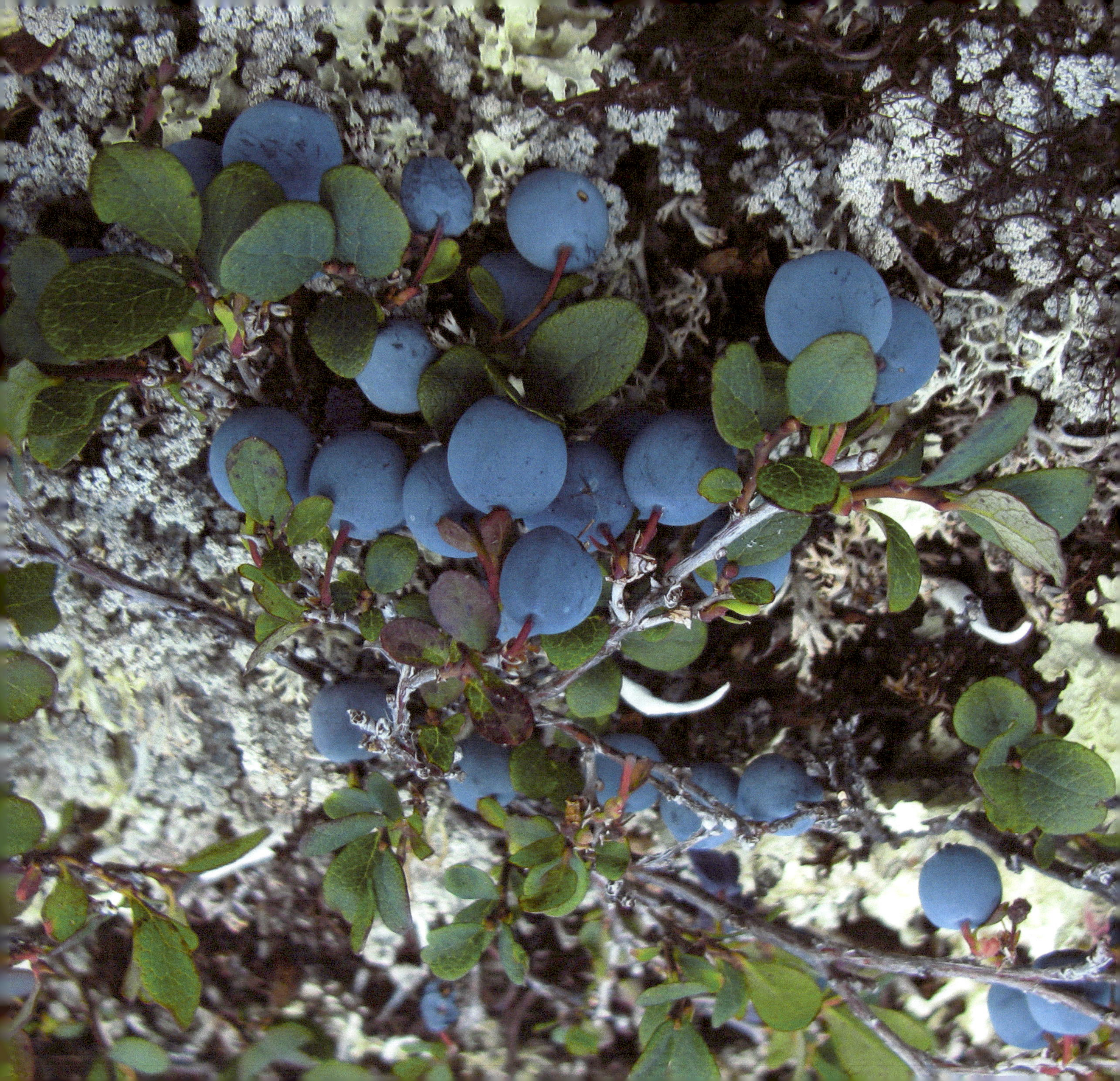

August 2018

Sun	Mon	Tue	Wed	Thu	Fri	Sat
29	30	31	1	2	3	4
5	6	7	8	9	10	11
12	13	14	15	16	17	18
19	20	21	22	23	24	25
	27	28	29	30	31	1

Vaccinium uliginosum (Blueberries) at Wickersham Dome near Fairbanks, Alaska.

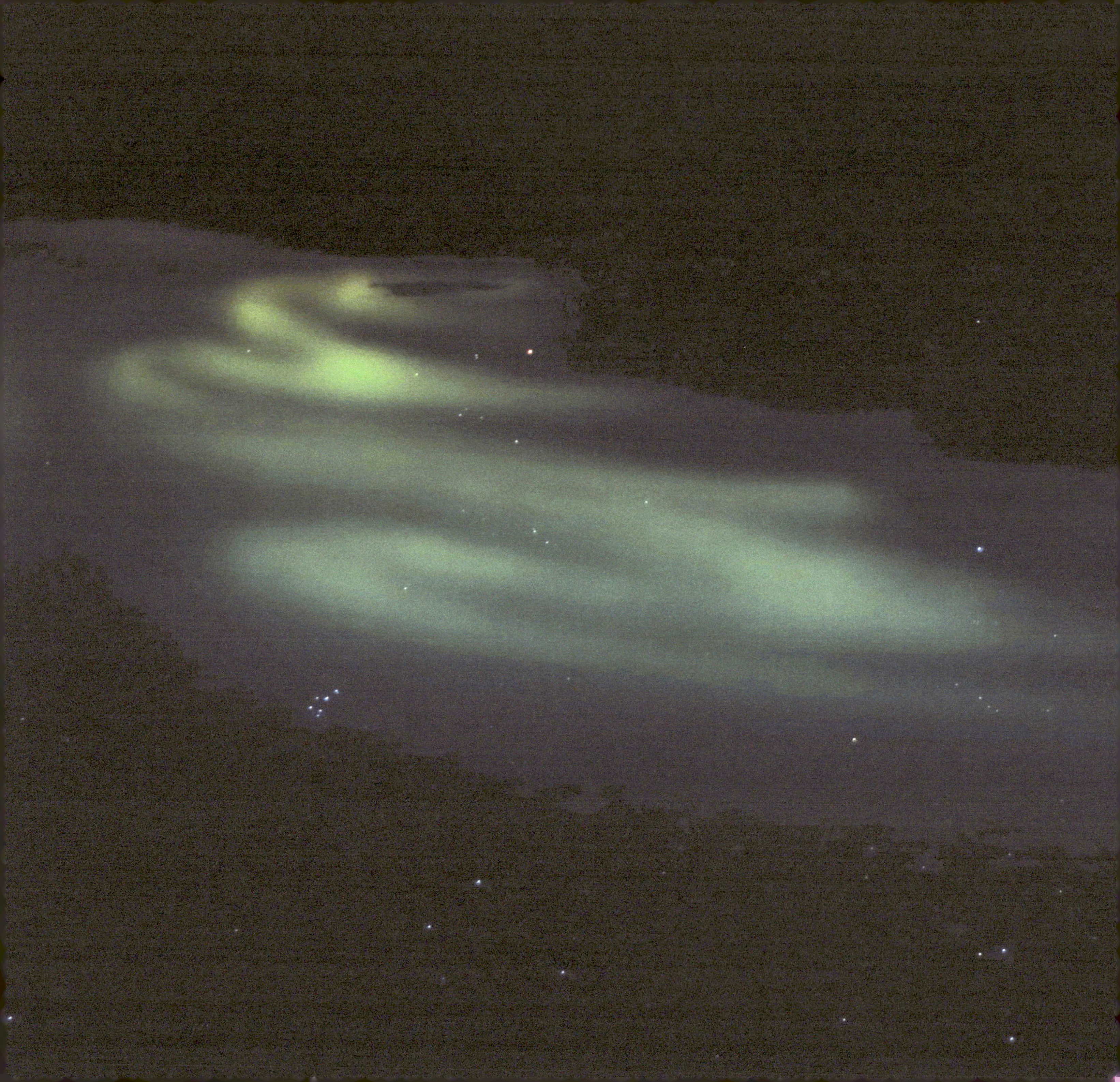

September 2018

Sun	Mon	Tue	Wed	Thu	Fri	Sat
26	27	28	29	30	31	1
2	3 Labor Day	4	5	6	7	8
9	10	11	12	13	14	15
16	17	18	19	20	21	22
23 01:54 GMT Autumnal Equinox	24	25	26	27	28	29
30	1	2	3	4	5	6

The Aurora Borealis, or Northern Lights near Fairbanks, Alaska.

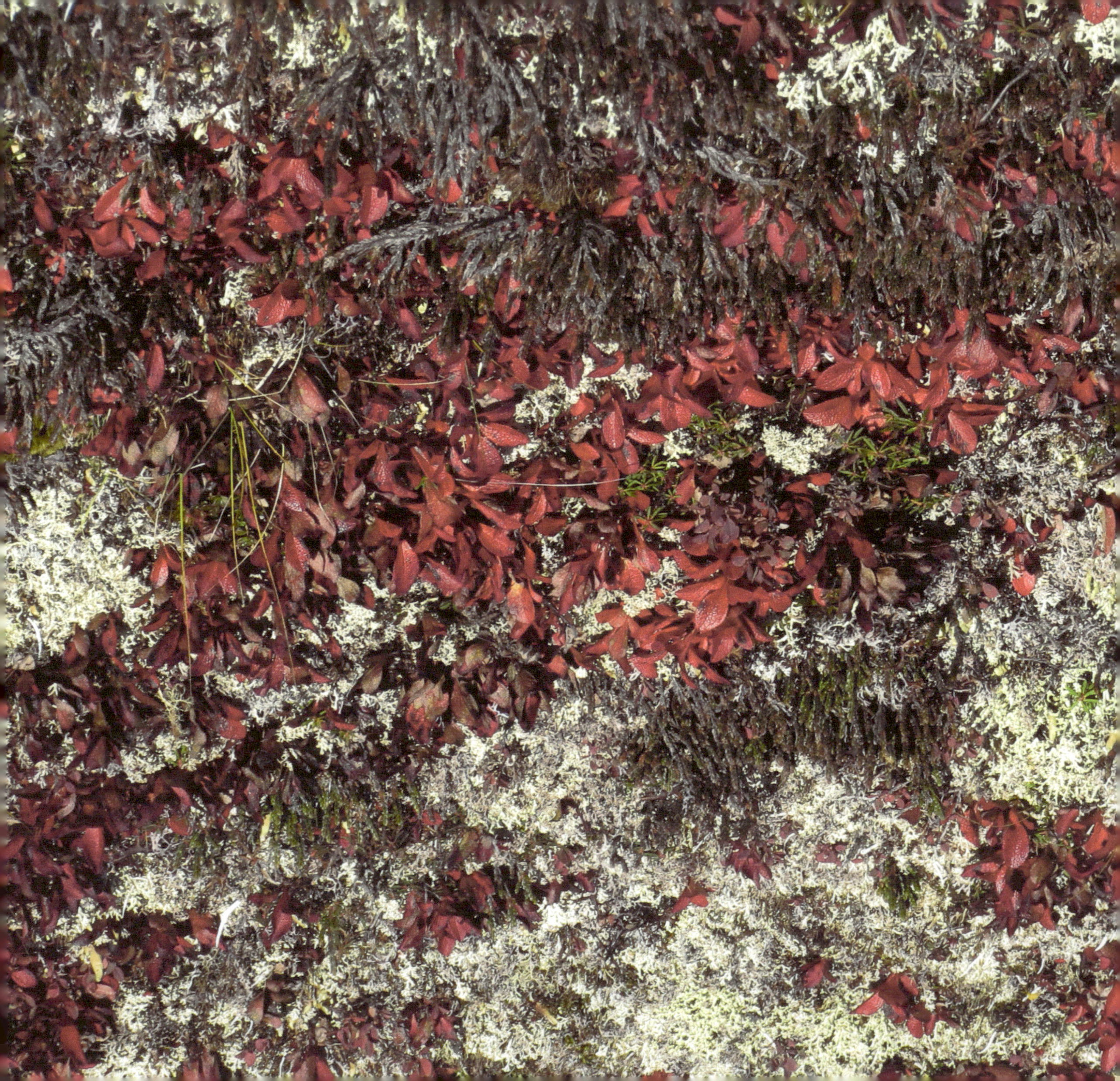

October 2018

Sun	Mon	Tue	Wed	Thu	Fri	Sat
30	1	2	3	4	5	6
7	8 Columbus Day	9	10	11	12	13
14	15	16	17	18	19	20
21	22	23	🌕	25	26	27
28	29	30	31 Halloween	1	2	3

Bearberry (*Arctostaphylos alpina*) on Wickersham Dome near Fairbanks, Alaska.

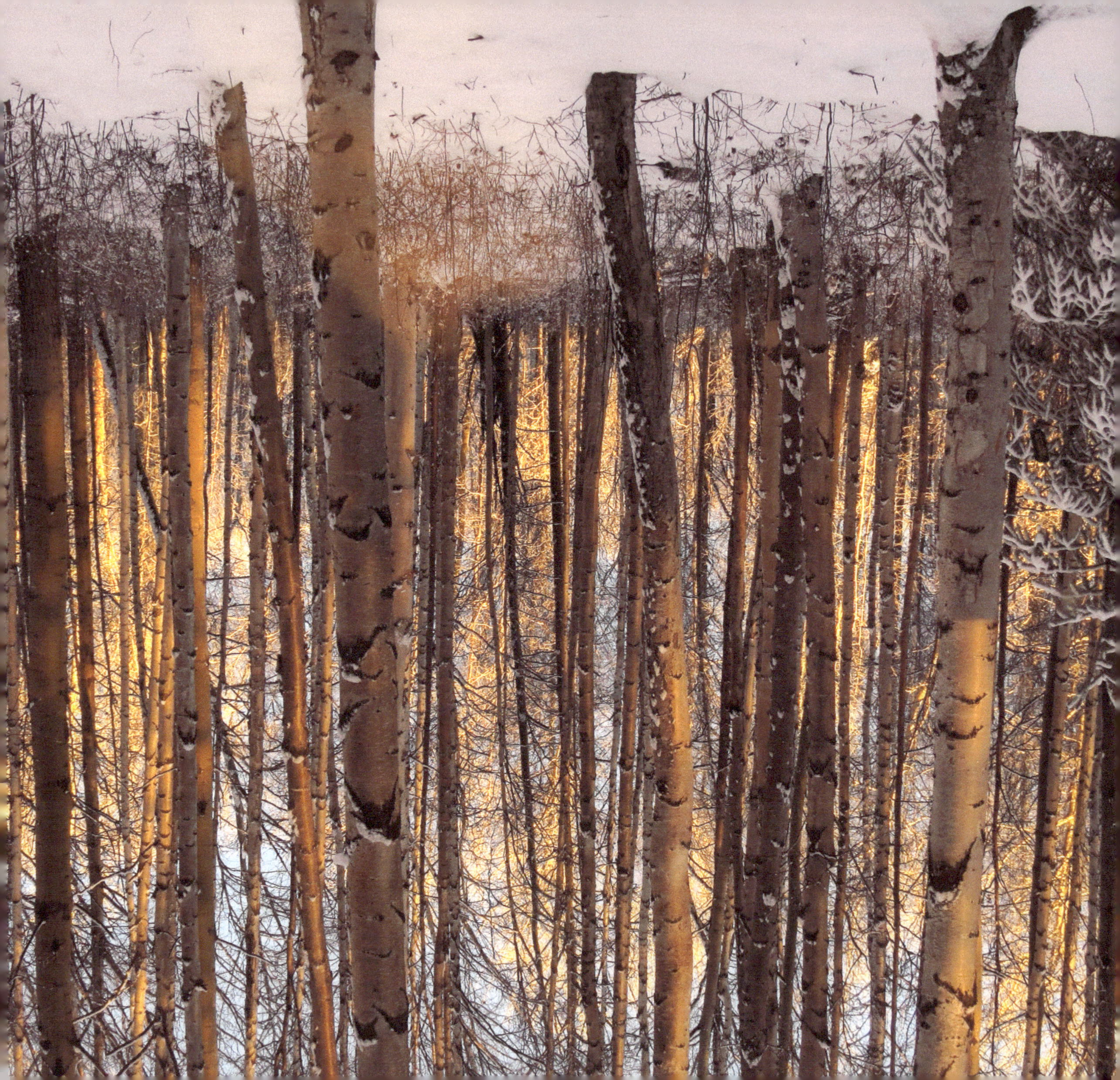

November 2018

Sun	Mon	Tue	Wed	Thu	Fri	Sat
28	29	30	31	1	2	3
4 Daylight Saving Time End (02:00)	5	6	7	8	9	10
11 Veteran's Day	12 Veteran's Day observed	13	14	15	16	17
18	19	20	21	22 Thanksgiving Day	23	24
25	26	27	28	29	30	1

An amazing November morning in the birch forest, Fairbanks, Alaska.

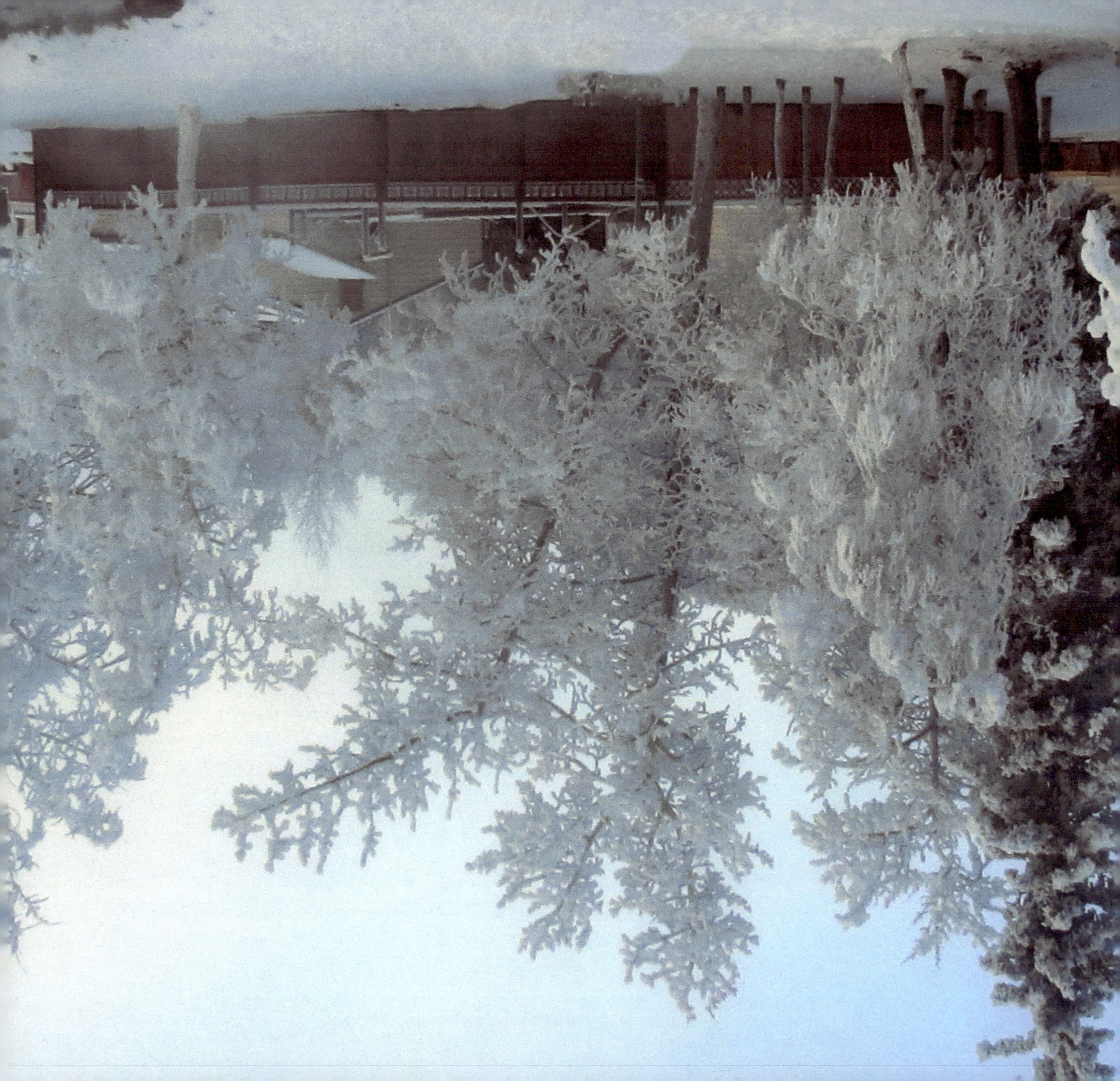

December 2018

Sun	Mon	Tue	Wed	Thu	Fri	Sat
25	26	27	28	29	30	1
2	3	4	5	6	7	8
9	10	11	12	13	14	15
16	17	18	19	20	21 22:22 GMT Winter Solstice	
23	24 Christmas Eve	25 Christmas Day	26	27	28	29
30	31 New Year's Eve	1	2	3	4	5

Chena Hot Springs Resort on a cold December morning, near Fairbanks, Alaska.

2018 Phases of the Moon

Universal Time (GMT)

	New Moon				First Quarter				Full Moon				Last Quarter		
	d	h	m		d	h	m		d	h	m		d	h	m
—	—	—	—	—	—	—	—	JAN	02	02	25	JAN	08	22	26
JAN	17	02	18	JAN	24	22	20	JAN	31	13	27	FEB	07	15	55
FEB	15	21	06	FEB	23	08	09	MAR	02	00	52	MAR	09	11	22
MAR	17	13	14	MAR	24	15	35	MAR	31	12	37	APR	08	07	21
APR	16	01	59	APR	22	21	46	APR	30	00	59	MAY	08	02	11
MAY	15	11	49	MAY	22	03	50	MAY	29	14	20	JUN	06	18	34
JUN	13	19	45	JUN	20	10	52	JUN	28	04	54	JUL	06	07	52
JUL	13	02	49	JUL	19	19	53	JUL	27	20	22	AUG	04	18	19
AUG	11	09	59	AUG	18	07	49	AUG	26	11	58	SEP	03	02	39
SEP	09	18	02	SEP	16	23	16	SEP	25	02	54	OCT	02	09	47
OCT	09	03	47	OCT	16	18	02	OCT	24	16	47	OCT	31	16	42
NOV	07	16	02	NOV	15	14	54	NOV	23	05	41	NOV	30	00	21
DEC	07	07	21	DEC	15	11	49	DEC	22	17	50	DEC	29	09	36

Earth's Seasons – 2018

Universal Time (GMT)

		d	h			d	h	m		d	h	m
Perihelion	Jan	03	05	Equinoxes	Mar	20	16	15	Sept	23	01	54
Aphelion	July	06	17	Solstices	June	21	10	07	Dec	21	22	22

If you enjoyed the photographs shown in this calendar then please be sure to check out our website. It can be found at http://danwiz.com. As long as he is alive he hopes to be able to maintain it.

Kazuya's blog can be found at: http://studiesofplantsandwildlife.blogspot.com or alternately, http://www2.blogger.com/profile/02622643778290337101.